"Sacrifice"

A stronger state of mind,
I don't need a title.

My domineer is a product
of applying to the Bible.

Never had an idol.
Blessing after blessing.

I'm not entitled,
but they're spiteful.

God promised dominion
over ALL my rivals,

& Eternal Life.
Chance after chance,
I'm trying to get it right.

Because son of man is wicked.
If we had a chance,
we'd do it twice.

God calls it corruption.
Son of man calls it "A way of life."

Not everything is beneficial.
Soon we'll have to pay the price.

But that's why God gave us a gift.

We call him Jesus Christ.

To wash away our sins,
He was tortured
& gave his precious life.

To save our place in paradise.
We know the truth & see the light.

Call it what you want,
but that was the ultimate sacrifice.

"Addiction." (Explicit)

Live learn and forget.
I can list a million reasons
why I'm sad or upset.

Why I'm self-aware, insecure,
& wayyy out of check.

Why I'm still so depressed.
Why I have nothing left.

All this damn anxiety
is just a stupid topic.

A broad range of symptoms.
Medication in my pocket.

Down seven pills,
like it isn't toxic.

Weak-minded, self-doubting,
& a bit nostalgic.

But I'm observant.
Everybody tries to lecture me,
& tell me what's the best for me.

Wondering what kinds of secrets
everyone has kept from me.

Cause Alcohol and drugs kind of help,
but they mess with me.

So trust me I appreciate
whoever really checks for me.

Put my cellphone down,
because too many people's texting me.

Business or personal,
I can never let it pressure me.

3 am, still awake,
wondering what's next for me.

So I just take another pill
& let it take effect on me.

"Adolescence." (Explicit)

See as a child,
I only opened up to a beat.

Ain't talk to nobody.
Shit, ain't nobody wanna talk to me.

Guess "antisocial" was an
understatement.

Whether that's cliché or opinion,
I ain't care what other kids where saying.

Tried to smile at girls that passed me by,
but it's hard when you're kind of shy.

Always walked away feeling stupid,
didn't know why.

Adderall in the morning.
Always went to school high.

Because socializing's always easier in
my mind.

Abnormal interest,
But idk, I guess that makes a guy a
geek.

Was never trendy.
Never had a checkmark on my sneaks.

Hypocritically if I had money, I had friends.

But I was always broke, so honestly it's a sad end.

Kind of is to this day.
Even though my saving's wayyyyy happier than it used to be back in the day.

I see some boobs then I get the urge to masterbate.

Then wipe it on my brother's shirt.
"Sibling powers, ACTIVATE!"

That nigga knew that now, he'd
probably catch a case.

Wings on the Little Tikes car, like it's a
wacky race.

Laughing at jokes, when I barely knew
the reference.

Just another 12 hours in Juanito's
adolescence.

"Mental Illness." (Explicit)

Self diagnostics.
I hate it.

Suicidal actions for attention?.
STOP FAKING!.

I want to end it real quick.
You don't comprehend the demons
that I deal with.

You want total sympathy,
when this is real shit.

I'm talking tears in my eyes.
I'm talking about the warfare that's
going on in my mind.

I'm talking 9 or 10 pills at a time.
I don't know if they're upset & I
don't know if they're fine.

Unfamiliar circumstance doesn't
give me butterflies.

It makes me fucking nauseous, & it
happens all the time.

Sometimes my only outlet is a pen.
So I'm begging you,

please stop treating mental illness
like it's a trend.

"Pros & Cons."

Okay. Yes my brain is big,
but my heart is even bigger.

& yes I have a temperament,
but only when it's triggered.

So try and tell me all my
imperfections.
I won't listen.

I decipher them myself.
It's irrelevant to list them.

From my perspective
it's just condescending criticism.

Although it may not be.
You're probably dropping wisdom.

My minds a bit chaotic
when I let it get to drifting.

Somehow I feel better
When there's something in my
system.

At the same time I hate it.
I wake up and I'm tripping.

Off balance, crystal vision,
dysfunctional decisions.

I can go on & on
about what's wrong with Juan.

But let's focus on the pros,
& forget about the cons.

"What's wrong?" (Explicit)

What's wrong kid? Nothing much.
Emotions and such.

Sometimes I'd rather take a shot than
sit and smoke a dutch.

Now a lot of people thing its wrong,
but I don't give a fuck.

Healthy coping mechanisms?
Nah I'd rather stay stuck.

Because everyone's hurt.
Dealing with some sort of baggage.

How the hell do I help you?
When I have my own damage.

My sudden waves of sadness.
My suicidal tantrums

It may sound a bit selfish,
but I'm only being candid.

I glorify the type of behavior
you find outlandish.

If you're odd then you're interesting,
so please raise your standards.

19.   *67

The softest hearts coming from the
hardest parts of Camden.

But I suppose a single soul wouldn't
understand it.

"The Pitts." (Explicit)

Survival of the fittest.
Better eat or be eaten.

In the trenches with some demons.
Black hearted, pure evil.

Disrespect them & they'll do you in.
Like that's a valid reason.

To be labeled "Real"
they would jeopardize their own
freedom.

But I don't sell rocks.

I don't fear any man who bleeds,
nor a cop.

So put that gun down
& put your hands up. Let's rock.

Or would you rather not?
Are you really a man
or rather hide behind a glock?

"Balance."

I've done seen darker nights
brighter days.

Try to fight these crappy feelings.
They bombard me anyway.

& kick my ass up & down.
Insecurity getting loud.

& it's drowning out every sound,
as I fade away in the crowd.

Because I care way too much about
what people think.

A like or a follow would put the
biggest smile on my face.

Turn off my phone.
Put it down.

Take a walk
& I look around.

Then I don't feel so bad,
because it's a beautiful day.

*9 7 8 1 7 9 4 7 7 4 7 4 2 *

Here we meet;

Let me start by telling you that you are normal, as a matter of fact you are not normal, yet incredible. By just investing your time into this book you are giving me the impression that you are a truly positive and motivated person.

I'd like to remind you of something, something perhaps familiar to you- phases. A phase is better known as a chapter in our very lives, although sometimes that chapter might well make us want to rip it out of the book.

A phase could conclude of a temporary change in attitude and Charisma or even simply a style we have recently adopted two and proceed to Later change back. At this point you might be thinking 'no way' in sarcasm or wondering what I'm trying to achieve here, but there is a certain type of reassurance you may not know you need; sometimes we might adapt personality traits that we are potentially oblivious to or even in denial of.

No matter your predicament whether you're investing your time into this book as a consequence of becoming someone you're not happy with being, having had a change which has distance you from people you typical Lee surround yourself with or even adapting to a star you feel out of place in, you will benefit from what I like to call 'the beauty of change'

Chapter one; The beauty of change

Changing is the most inevitable action of our very existence. When we are young we tend to make many mistakes in which we quite literally grow from although what people forget is this continuously applies whether the term becomes metaphorical or for the reason that we literally never stop growing.

What makes this difficult to process is the fact that harshly, as we grow our minds grow alongside us, as our minds grow we become more brutal, Judgemental and many of us worry what our every little action or thought might say about us as a person or what in which we have become.

The truth is most mistake don't define who you are no phase, no intrusive thoughts and no temporary attitude - Lucky for you a phase so simple to overcome as no one is better at being you more than you are.

Do me a favour, ask yourself "am I the person I want to be? ", "Do I put others before myself? ", "Do I tend to forget things that I obliviously do could to the weight on someone's shoulders?" And if your answers result in disappointment and a melancholy feeling I would like you to do one more thing; Surround yourself with that ongoing feeling of guilt, dissatisfaction and disappointment and just tense. As you release banish those very thoughts and smile with relief knowing you're one step closer to being the person you're proud to be because as my beautiful mother once told me "everyone is entitled to a strop "

Chapter two; Unrequited

You may be familiar with the term unrequited, possibly due to the many previous feelings and predicament you have experienced relating to the word – or perhaps hearing the word instigates your memory of the tragedy of Romeo and Juliet or even quite simply the many times you've been taking for granted, given your all to receive nothing in return.

You potentially can't make sense of how unappreciated you are what you have done to deserve this feeling of this regard. But let me change your mindset one which will provide you with pleasure, satisfaction and an undeniable sense of pride.

When feeling a sense of unrequited love you are not to feel for yourself not receiving what you give yet you are to feel for the person taking from you and appreciate how lucky you are that you are gifted with such consideration and the talent of putting yourself in someone else's shoes, because let me tell you, that, evidently, is one beautiful trait.

Chapter three; muscles of the mind

What do muscles portray? Strength. Source. Power. The power of your mind is the biggest bicep to exist, with the ability to lift your mood , your emotions, your motivation alongside your physical state – whilst also having equal ability to drop them right back down again.

 Nothing can mess you up for more than your own mind can ,or,, in better words, "nothing will work unless you do ".

The world adapts to how we choose to see it, with hope and aspiration it seems full of ongoing opportunities however once our mind rebels the positive thoughts this world can become cruel and , as a cliché, dark. We are not to blame the world for this bipolar, but our very minds.

Picture yourself in a better place and motivate yourself to get there – you'll be amazed at what you attract once you start believing in what you deserve.

So motivate yourself to grow this muscle into the strongest, most obedient bicep, and you will find yourself in a better place as once you're mind chooses hope and aspiration, you will be provided with the most overwhelming sense of power you can imagine, as what you can imagine is what you can achieve.

"The most confused we get is when we attempt to convince our heads of something our hearts know is a lie"- Karen Moning

"Don't treat people how they treat you, treat them how you wish they treated you"

"Be the moon and inspire people, even when you're far from full"-K.tolnoe

"Your limitations are defined by your imagination"-Tony Robins

"Be steady in the soul, and free in the spirit"-Butterflies rising

"Don't believe another can complete you, when you are capable of completing yourself; only believe that one can motivate you to do so"

"If you were born with the weakness to fall you were born with the strength to rise"- Rupi Kaur

"She has a galaxy in her eyes and a universe in her mind"-Rosie Perry

"What matters most is how well you walk through fire"-Charles Bukowski

"Be patient and tough; someday
This pain will be useful
To you"-Ovid

"You'll stop hurting believe me. You'll Stop hurting the day you fall in love with someone who has the same meaning of love as you"

-you'll stop hurting

"Never allow yourself to second guess what's first on your heart" – Nerd creative

"If you have been brutally broken, but still have the courage to be gentle to others then you deserve a love deeper than the ocean itself" -Nikita Gill

And most importantly ...
*   "Everyone's entitled to a strop"*